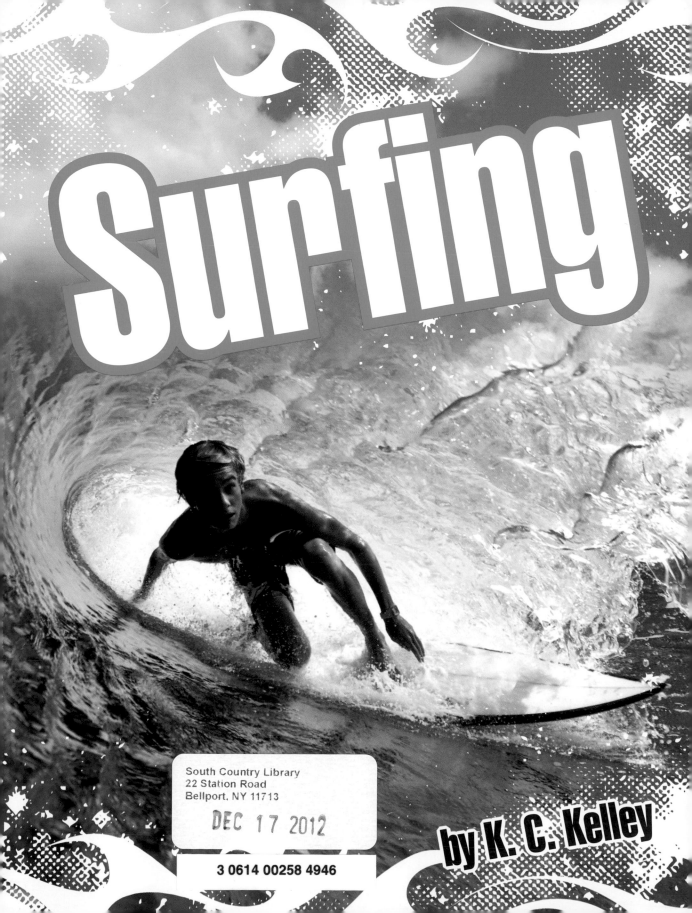

Surfing

by K. C. Kelley

Published by The Child's World®
1980 Lookout Drive
Mankato, MN 56003-1705
800-599-READ
www.childsworld.com

The Child's World®: Mary Berendes, Publishing Director
Shoreline Publishing Group, LLC: James Buckley Jr.,
    Production Director
The Design Lab: Design and production

ISBN: 978-1-60973-185-4
LCCN: 2011928875

Photo credits: Cover: iStock.
Interior: AP/Wide World: 8, 20; Corbis: 4, 24, 27, 28;
dreamstime.com: Paul Topp 11, Brian Finestone 12,
Marc Prefontaine 15, Francois De Ribaucourt 16,
Epicstock 19; iStock: 23; North Wind Archives: 7.

Printed in the United States of America
Mankato, Minnesota
July, 2011
PA02094

Table of Contents

Laird Hamilton challenged one of the world's biggest waves.

CHAPTER ONE

Surfing a Mountain of Water

It's a sunny day in August, 2000, near the South Pacific island of Tahiti. In the ocean, a wave rises up like a giant blue wall. The front of the wave is as high as a five-story building. As the surf roars and the wave grows, a small figure surfs down the front of the wave.

Laird Hamilton was that surfer. He was making history that day. No one thought such giant waves could be surfed safely. Hamilton took that dare and beat the wave. He was crowned the king of the "big-wave surfers."

Not every surfer has to wait for waves as high as buildings. On waves big and small, millions of people enjoy surfing. This exciting water sport of riding waves mixes **ancient** skills and modern boards. It has also helped create new fashion and music.

No one knows when surfing began. Pacific islanders have been riding waves on wooden boards for centuries. English sailors first saw surfing in the 1700s. The sport didn't catch on anywhere else until Hawaiians brought it to the United States early in the 20th century. People in California looking for water thrills began to surf, too. Australians caught on soon as well.

Ancient Hawaiians were the first to try surfing.

The Duke

One Hawaiian is given credit for helping bring surfing to the U.S. Duke Kahanamoku was a surfer and star swimmer. He competed in five Olympic Games, earning gold medals in swimming. He used his fame to bring his native sport of surfing to the U.S. Duke **demonstrated** surfing in California and other places. He was the first person to be in the Surfing Hall of Fame and the Swimming Hall of Fame.

The sport remained small and local until the 1960s, however. That's when large, wooden boards gave way to boards made of a type of plastic called polyurethane. "Poly" boards could be smaller and lighter. They were easier to carry, ride, and learn on. People called "shapers" were able to carve new styles of surfboard for all sorts of people. Almost overnight, surfing caught on in a big way on coasts around the world.

With the sport came new fashion, inspired by the beach. People who lived far from oceans wore flip-flops first worn by surfers, as well as surf shorts and Hawaiian shirts. In the 1960s, "surf guitar" music gave teenagers a great new way to dance. The famous Beach Boys rock band spread the music around the world. A famous movie called *Endless Summer* followed a group of surfers as they chased waves around the world.

This scene from a surf movie shows how the sport first came to California beaches.

For most surfers, the sport is a way to connect to the ocean. They surf not to win or beat the other surfers but to just to surf. Other surfers want to show their stuff against others. An international pro surfing group holds contests around the world. (Read more about the best in Chapter 3.)

While most surfers find waves to ride near their homes, others, like Hamilton take on the challenge of the big waves.

Now, let's go surfing!

This surfer is cutting down the face, or front, of the wave.

Putting wax on the surfboard makes sure feet get a good grip on the wet board.

CHAPTER TWO

Hit the Surf!

A surfer needs just two things to surf: waves and a surfboard. They find the waves on beaches around the world. They get a choice of surfboards, too.

The most popular type of surfboard is a shortboard. Surfers choose the height and width of the board based on their own size and skill. Smaller, narrower boards are for experts. Taller, wider boards can be better for newer surfers. Shortboards are great for doing turns and quick moves on the waves.

Some surfers choose to ride longboards. Made of poly, they are still more like the old wooden boards used by ancient Hawaiians. Longboards can't turn as well, but can give surfers a longer ride.

Surfers rub wax atop each of these types of boards. The wax gives their feet a grip. The type of wax used changes depending on the weather.

Plastic fins on the bottom of surfboards help them steer. Early longboards didn't have fins. When they were added, it gave surfers more control. Some boards now have two or three fins.

Most beginners use a foamboard. These have a softer cover and are lightweight. The foam helps "grab" the water and makes learning easier. The soft cover also prevents injuries if the surfer or others are hit by the board.

Another way to prevent "runaway" surfboards is with a leash. The surfer puts a Velcro collar on his ankle with a rubber cord attached to the board. When he falls off, the board won't drift away. Some surfers also wear helmets for protection in case of falls or from being bonked with others' boards. In cold water, surfers can wear wetsuits to keep warm while they surf.

A rubber leash keeps the surfboard from floating away.

The first step to surfing is paddling out to find a good wave.

With all the gear in hand, it's time to hit the waves. Classes and schools can help people learn to surf. Most surfers also learn from family members.

Here are the basic moves to catching a wave. Lying chest-down on the board, paddle with your hands as the wave rushes up behind you. As it catches the board, you stand up quickly. One foot should be in front of the other as you crouch down. (If you choose to put your left foot in front, you're a "goofy-foot" in surf talk.) Keep your balance as the wave rushes forward. As you improve, you learn to turn the board by shifting your weight or moving your feet.

Of course, sometimes surfers fall off a wave. That's called a "wipeout." But every surfer knows that once you fall off . . . you just climb back on and wait for the next wave.

When choosing that wave, surfers look for a good **face** (or front of the wave) to ride on. They watch where the waves are breaking. They want a wave that will not break too soon or else their ride will be very short. Talented surfers watch for waves that break in a long, rolling curve called a barrel. Riding such a wave so that the barrel is above the surfer is a great thrill. Coming out the other side is called "shooting the curl."

Shooting the curl is one of the coolest rides a surfer can take.

A surfer on a Jet Ski waits his turn to be towed in to giant waves like this one.

Surf Talk
Surfing has a language all its own. Here are some of the words that surfers use in their sport:
barrel—the inside of a long, curving wave
grommet—a young surfer
hang ten—to stand with all ten toes over the front edge of the board
outside—where surfers look for the next waves
set—a group of waves that come one after the other
soup—the foamy white water formed after a wave breaks near shore
stick—a surfboard
wipeout—fall off the board while surfing

Skilled surfers can surf waves up to 10 or 15 feet. However, it takes skill and courage to tackle the giant waves like Hamilton. In recent years, these huge waves were surfed with help from jet-skis. Human power can paddle fast enough to get ahead of these waves. So jet-skis tow the surfers in, then zoom out of the way.

Surfing is an ancient sport, but people are still finding new ways to hit the waves.

CHAPTER THREE

Surf Stories

What is the biggest wave ever surfed? That's actually hard to say. Waves don't exactly stand still to get measured. Some experts say a 75–85 foot (23–26 m) wave far off southern California in 2008 was the biggest. Others point to waves south of San Francisco as bigger. The wave Laird Hamilton rode in Tahiti in 2000 was 50 feet or so. Not the biggest, but the first big-wave ride captured on film.

While surfers such as Laird Hamilton rule the big waves. Kelly Slater is the king of the rest of them. Slater has won an amazing 10 world championships.

Wipeouts in giant waves can be very dangerous.

Kelly Slater shows off his amazing kick turn move.

He competes on the ASP (Association of Surfing Professionals) Tour. The ASP Tour started in 1976 to give surfers a way to compete. Judges on the beach give points to surfers for tricks, length of ride, and style. Winners of events earn points toward an annual championship.

Slater grew up in Florida and was a surf-contest winner by the time he was eight. In 1992, he was the youngest to win the world title. He was 20. Then he won five straight from 1994 to 1998. After taking some time off to do other things (including movies), he returned to the waves. Though younger surfers challenged him, he was still the champ. At 33 in 2005, he was the oldest surfer to win the title. Amazingly, he kept on winning. In 2010, he captured his 10th career world championship. Slater is simply the best overall surfer ever.

He faces challenges on the ASP Tour from around the world. Taj Burrows and Mick Fanning grew up surfing in Australia's warm waters. Victor Ribas learned to surf in his **native** Brazil. Jordy Smith, the **runner-up** to Slater in 2010, comes from South Africa.

Women are great surfers, too. The women's pro tour started in 1977. The Kelly Slater of the women's tour is Australia's Layne Beachley. She won seven world titles before retiring in 2008. Fellow **Aussie** Stephanie Gilmore is going after Layne's record. Stephanie won the title in 2010 for the fourth straight time. The woman known as "Happy" for her great smile won her first title when she was only 17!

Layne Beachley was one of the best female surfers ever.

River Surfing?
People who live away from beaches look for waves, too. The flow of some rivers in Germany and in the Pacific Northwest creates a wave. It doesn't move forward like an ocean wave. It stays in one place. Surfers can jump in and ride for a long time, staying mostly in one place!

27

Stephanie Gilmore has won four world titles.

Other top world stars include Sofia Mulanovich from Peru and Silvana Lima from Brazil. The top U.S. surfer on the 2010 women's tour was Carissa Moore. She grew up in Hawaii, one of the homes of surfing.

From big waves to small, for trophies or just for fun, surfing is a great sport for people who love the ocean. For most surfers, the greatest joy is not the perfect wave or a big win, but just floating on their board, watching the sun sparkle the blue waters.

Glossary

ancient—centuries old . . . or more

Aussie—nickname for a person from Australia

demonstrated—showed how to do something

face—in surfing, the front of a wave as it faces the beach

native—an adjective used to show where a person was born

runner-up—a person who finishes second in a contest

BOOKS

Catching Waves
By Matt Christopher and Stephanie Peters. New York, NY: Little Brown Books for Young Readers, 2010.
This novel tells the story of surf kid Kai Ford and the lessons he learns about surfing and life.

Kelly Slater
By Jeff Young. Greensboro, NC: Morgan Reynolds, 2009.
Slater is the world's greatest surfer. This book tells his life story.

Surf's Up!
By K.C. Kelley. Mankato, MN: The Child's World, 2009.
Meet the best surfers in the world and read more about how they became champions.

WEB SITES

For links to learn more about extreme sports: **childsworld.com/links**

Note to Parents, Teachers, and Librarians: We routinely verify our Web links to make sure they are safe and active sites. So encourage your readers to check them out!

Index

About the Author

K. C. Kelley lives right up the street from a great surf spot in Santa Barbara, California. He has written books for young readers about baseball, football, and soccer, as well as about animals, astronauts, and other cool stuff.